TELLING TIME BY THE SHADOWS

TELLING TIME BY THE SHADOWS

poems

J.M. FitzGerald

TURNING POINT

Telling Time by the Shadows

©2008 J.M. FitzGerald

Published by Turning Point
P.O. Box 541106
Cincinnati, OH 45254-1106

Typeset in Goudy by Michael Vukadinovich

ISBN: 9781934999035
LCCN: 20089243000

Poetry Editor: Kevin Walzer
Business Editor: Lori Jareo

Visit us on the web at www.turningpointbooks.com

ACKNOWLEDGMENTS

Prayer parts 1 and 3 appeared in *Illuminations: Expressions of the Personal Spiritual Experience*
Thanks to Mark L. Tompkins and Jennifer McMahon.

Adjusting the Loneliness first appeared in *The Center for American Artists*
Many thanks to James and Jules White for their encouragement.

Aphrodite, Flying Lessons, My Addiction and *Prayer* parts 1 and 5
were broadcast on KPFK Pacifica Radio, *The Poet's Café*.
Special thanks to host Michael "MC" Bruce and producer Marlena Bond.

Heartfelt thanks to Elena Karina Byrne, for her gracious promotion of my work.

Thanks to Mike Vukadinovich, for all his help.

Thanks to D'Lynn Waldron, for all her help.

Cover art: *September Sunset, Avebury* by Jane Tomlinson
www.janetomlinson.com

Author Photo: Hélène Cardona

For Hélène, with all my love.
Without her, these poems would not have been possible.

CONTENTS

I

Three Blue Years and a Light One

II

Where God is Really a Woman

III

Involve Me in Happenings

IV

Humbled

V
The Title Lied

I
THREE BLUE YEARS AND A LIGHT ONE

If I had only known, I would have been a locksmith.
—Albert Einstein

THE MISUNDERSTOOD

As for the talking,
if I wanted something said,
it would be here.

These lines exist as they do for the falling,
for the unrevealed hurt,
for God to cry and angels fear

at my corruption,
at my shaking,
at my curse.

I need time to get away,
but present demons love me worse,
and figure ways to pose as muses.

They point to where my secrets wither.
They bruise the heights and stir the lows
with longing songs that ever crave to scream:

Let me come back!
No voice is greater than this.
What happened to the blasted silence?

No one should believe I'm real.
I disclaim myself for persona,
or I'd be bawling.

The poem is over,
I used to feel.
But now who knows?

Talking to Rilke

I see you know loneliness, wanting not just words,
but verse to sprinkle mystery on the breeze
and feed the page, as if every moment
is observed and respected for its holiness.
And it is unique not just because of itself,
but because of its unity with you,
transcending either in its wholeness.

Then there is the sound life makes,
as if its shadow passed,
it mourns every loss to rejoice every birth.
For in the land where shadows go it must be dark
inasmuch as they mingle.

A phantom flashes on the wall, and startles—
is something crawling? Just the wind.
Don't get killed when you're in love.
Because you didn't when you were alone.

Loneliness is always waiting.
Waiting for touches, tones, arrivals.
Waiting for worlds to fill the page.
Waiting at the dusky outskirts,
like a lion crouched in patient approach,
with a stare so intense it burns your back.

And loneliness waits as it does for existence,
to become what it must when nothing is left.
Don't run. You have no choice but be one with it,
recognize it as yourself with nowhere else to go.

A theme begins to unfold, exposed.
Still, so as not to be noticed.
Keep your back turned till the end.
No lion can bear the face of a poet.
Even the cover photo stares back,

reminds me how we all crave fire.
So I laugh, and cover your face with this page,
its words now a hundred times their size, reverse
our void with a universe, no longer waiting.

MAGUS

I would be one of the wanderers,
with heaven watching.
Observe, you reflections, I glance away.

Notice the wonder spring forth in ancientness,
steep the spell held in spices, hypnotized.
In dreams I descend twenty steps at a time,

am afraid how I'll land if I fly too high.
I try not to say I, and claim myself,
a sign of consciousness uncovering.

Who calls me, from such transience?
We will ourselves into vastness,
like children at graves,

a wind with just one chance to blow,
both toward and away from itself in surprise,
or life is waste.

There are shooting stars, then that which lingers,
even hovers like a hawk, a halo, a messenger.
None can bear looking straight into the sun.

We see it reflect off the ocean by day, the moon at night.
Imagine someone's sun fly away.
What must it search for, in its burning?

Galaxies witness it bursting through silence.
May it hover to the end in spite of where it finds itself.
Let innocence cling to the universe, swirling,

get high and go hungry, distill our minds
till we can't control what pours from inside,
and at heart remain addicts, ever humble.

APHRODITE

For a good group of words, take the night,
and let it unfold into such a very simple thing
as is impossible to hear,
like rain at a distance, or shore from a cliff.
I've forgotten how I feel,
as if run through by light,
I find no further truths.

Attune to air, where sound dwells a moment,
its waves boiled down to an instant, anointed in me.
For days now I have pictured silence
as something meaningful, a story in and of itself.

There, in the loneliness, should be a song,
and here, right here, could go murmurs
or whispers of footsteps forever.

I walk by the ocean where no flowers grow,
because they couldn't bear the beauty.
I find a white stone that was a mountain when I was a star.
It reminds me we'll all be sand one day, so I let go,
but we are moved.

Then this woman wades in the tide.
She is part of the sunset, the clouds, the ocean.
The whole horizon wraps around her,
sending me telepathic thoughts of wonder and hope,
till I can't help but listen for God.

II
WHERE GOD IS REALLY A WOMAN

A man can stand anything except a succession of ordinary days.
　　　　　　　　　　　　　　—Johann Wolfgang von Goethe

PRAYER

1.
Now, I stare into emptiness,
alone enough for poetry,
alone enough for even me,
alone requiring mention of passing.

There are these words, a sound,
an order, evasive emotions
I've known so long, just not acknowledged.
But others begin to notice frozen souls.

I don't know why I seem surprised.
I'm making life happen, I let it run wild.
I ought to rein it in a little,
maybe do some real work.

Give me that alpha rhythmic vibe
and I'll go one-on-one with God.
God is not too busy for people like me.
I say, you are no God without me.

2.
God's not your name, it's a word—you are generic.
I'm generic too, with consequence.
You are the blankness I'm talking to,
and I am a man who is cold.

Sometimes mention of you means me,
a matter of context, or mood, even so,
I am more than you—
small g, capital I.

I am writer,
you are written.
God or not, you'd let me ignore you,
like everybody else does.

3.
You are words
to be written,
and I am here now.
Just stay there being nothing,

like a cipher, irreducible,
while I describe the sound
as a question worthy of presupposing
how it comes and goes.

You are a story with no facts,
a line at a time.
I don't even notice you go,
you return so fast.

You are a lonely aging man
who calls a grandchild
and wonders when he's coming back.
I'm like that too, not needing to believe.

4.
I utter prayers about you.
Though these too will be lines some day.
Maybe, when I say I don't believe,
it's because I really know.

I'm just waiting for words to mean themselves,
thinking of ways to rub you, get my wishes.
But waves and foam are what they are.
They never come true.

People tell me I think too much,
but I never know what that means.
I don't think I think too much.
I may even confuse it with feeling.

5.
You're greater than most, I'm afraid.
Your voice overflows,
becomes my surroundings,
across edges of spectra intense fascination.

I fly into sun, disintegrate,
let you keep the pieces, hard as reality.
Arrange them in any order you like.
Adrift, you are the oars that shatter silence,

the faintest breeze which stirs the sails,
the palm upon the poet's page.
Tiny thoughts know secret places,
you've somehow gotten into me

and rearranged sensation.
Dangled my vision into oblivion.
No chance to stop and be me, let's hope.
Hours drag into a fraction I forget I am alone.

I follow your flute across fissures of stone,
ripple at you skipping over me,
scatter like vapor before a gale,
souls you touch become the dawn.

6.
So connected to your rhythm,
I have to turn away,
or you would know me.
I feel you drawing secrets from my eyes.

Thought interrupts the flow of being
in a vacuum I ache to describe.
Fragrance and chimes float on the breeze,
pry presence open to stir up the line.

I give myself away in pieces,
as much as I can without falling apart,
that you, if you're there, can atone for desire.
Do it back to me.

See, there are truths I cannot count.
I am particles, so much tinier than life,
blown by a voice across mythical spaces,
like a history never told.

There is such sacrifice in oneness.
These words don't know how to explain.
They hate to divulge too much at once,
cast aside the veil of creation

and cling to a need for revelation.
If this moment has a name,
I am alone on earth and call it,
to hear you echo through my seashell like an ocean.

7.

I owe poetry, and know it.
Were I bardic,
how you'd swoon to my delight.
I'd get to the point then go on.

Confuse my lust with parts that yearn,
I am divided.
Should dust on artifacts be me, let's haunt them both,
foretelling momentary futures.

I believe I can make time. Ha! A dreamer!
The recipe is wisp and blows away.
I feel your reflection, the bass of your star.
It's the height one falls from that causes the glow.

8.

God, put your blood on the line.
Let your bones fill this whiteness.
Sacrifice rhyme to resurrect us.
Especially from the dead, I love that.

Tears still creep, erode my face.
I see in the mirror
your gaze burn back,
so in you I am still a child.

Just like any other word you've ever spoken,
I defer to the ultimate silence.
Actual truth would be cliché,
I am afraid to know.

I'm gathering particles, retracing patterns.
Strange how we return to night,
how it never stops changing,
until in the end we mean what we say.

9.
God is a breath coming out of me,
I'm a breath going back in.
Together, we comprise a moment lost forever,
and that's the only forever there is.

Hope is a feeling none should inspire,
but reality hurts, so we dream anything
to stay unconscious and get by.
Don't hang on. Let go. Let go.

Even love gets something out of itself.
Breaks rules and be free, however entwined.
Imagine, and I exist countless times.
I'll imagine you too, till we are whole.

10.
Distract me from the light, reflecting off you.
Make me mindful of a counterpart.
Can one possess this?
When you have it all, do you really have anything?

Let us practice what Gods and poets do,
this sort of craving, each instance I create you.
Circle the thoughts coming troubled and hard.
Then you are here in my unreasonable mind.

I project you into smiling places
of infinite glitter, and tinsel-singed darkness.
An utter bemusement in which I hope to glisten.
One gust from your wings lifts me over the moat.

11.

There is a ringing I wish I could make for you.
Truth, each generates inside,
Stands at the spigot and lets it flow.
Your secret me, how you count it among weeds.

And I know who plucked the tunes,
which I relay, oh yes, conception changes.
It moves because of you, swerves like water into cages.
Ooh, it caves me, even better than if the mind were mine.

A sound, I say, affects nerve.
I hear it tear and just keep groping.
Seems I'm not so godless after all.
Is this why you aren't afraid?

Glance down, and shores are depleted,
yet their waves keep bouncing back, and wasting.
You are the skyline that makes me ambitious.
The lonely one who reads me dreams.

12.
Overwhelm me.
I won't stop if you won't.
Keep climbing though the thunder rolls.
I'll check to see whether you're breathing,

lose touch with imagination,
be torn to pieces for an inkling.
Here's what you would see in me:
right now, its secrets too, bend reality

till the big thoughts pour down.
I have phrases and this is the night
with the ring of a star scrape.
I notice which wonder of the world we are.

Keep the goals just out of reach, in case.
I'll hear sounds, as if intended,
cause I'm on overdrive, and waning.
The wait has to end soon, sure as rope.

13.
I see no use drowning in me.
I too, am over myself.
No longer a dive through illusion into solid cold.
Step on my fingers and let me fall.

Where there is no fire, all ice sounds alike.
Two steps forward, two back, like nothing new.
God, we breathe near to one another.
Long as heaven hangs on, I won't let go.

It's painful, so long a drop,
and the skipping stone is soon for the bottom.
So fade into silence, leave night to ponder.
No one hears these words without you.

14.

A heart is more than a beat,
more than pulse, or the sum of its parts.
Forget the heart, I'm after yearning,
and am not sure what that makes me.

I give you time to run away, but you don't.
Instead you become invisible,
so I resort to other senses.
I know you are there, I feel the quaking.

Distances shrink, colors fade, oceans drain,
and then there's only you and I.
Where will you turn?
Trading souls with you is painful.

We are the moment's creator,
the only two who recognize it.
And if that isn't love, it's something more perfect,
that makes us whole.

15.
You've got me believing.
Let me warm you a little, what could it hurt?
Become is the wish of a dreamer, and yet,
I stumble upon you.

Your dawn, yes, your dawn escalates into night,
where vision leaves me weak, beyond, relax, relax.
Come back, but to life, what can I say?
Forever is late, and tomorrow awaiting.

Press escape. This is your chance.
I like it because it's later, and I still am.
Understand my absolute truth:
this moment, accept that it's gone.

16.
I wake for a voice
to savor long after, like cinders.
Mingle with being, come some pure way,
until even the aching feel young.

How do I get through an hour?
I'll be writing, or in the mindstream, with an image,
where a thought can penetrate a body.
Distract me from the hours again.

Forget which self we run wild in,
loose constellations to dots unconnected,
sacrifice these idols every line,
let them uncoil and draw back together,

blackout the tonic scenes for a vision
and sprain every notion.
For the weary with a spell, sheep count themselves.
Let us double each other then run out of room.

17.
Something comes before this.
I am impatient—these are the clues:
you're supposed to be miles away,
not here within me.

I'll be scrapping the pages, as usual, welling.
These got through.
It wasn't what I wanted to say.
Just what's left.

There is more to be revealed.
I have questions about myself,
and dreams are never hard enough to touch.
For now though, that's where I see you.

18.

(A Far Cry From Heaven)
Kiss me with your universe.
For you I'd turn a thousand phrases,
delve into their depths for secrets,
open the doors to all my dark places.

Bring your lines of candlelight
and let me cup my hands around them.
I'll protect your warmth from the wind,
we can wander to end of night.

I have enough life for us both to bleed,
pry pain from each finger to raise as my own.
This is my share of you, breeze and scent,
wrenching through me like a hole.

I'm mumbling to myself again.
Sparks from the corner of your eye
melt me two shades of blue,
so I can't help but fall.

Like a stone enamored by ocean,
I dive into a prayer of flight,
with such ghostlike wings as never open,
before waking at the bottom, broken.

Speak your soundless words to the hopeless,
in a vision too vast for me to behold.
Move me from here to there, like a poet.
Use the breath you took from me as potion.

19.
I'm guide to no one,
make little of me—
nothing's quieter than when God speaks.
Oh, to belong to mythology, be so inclined.

Swap me those lines I'd lie to write
and I'll keep asking nicer.
I'm almost hurt, can hardly turn my head,
but it's looking up, toward blue.

Predict me, and I'll live an instant.
Give me, in essence, a beginning.
For those upon earth, it is me.
There was never a time it wasn't.

20.
With a look, you calm the guardians.
For your voice they put down their shields,
come out of cloud shadow
plucking bowstrings like a harp.

When I imagine your horizon,
all I see is that much farther,
into solid sky where it fathoms the ocean.
As the Sun is a star, God is an angel.

It realizes self in time,
comes to matter in the universe.
These words are symbols
that heaven and earth remember what they started.

21.
I love that you apprehend the silence,
as if I could reveal myself in sound.
We walk like an old couple
through a garden of quiet understanding.

Mountains and ocean form one another,
devouring sun on the water bends
to where people say it doesn't get any better.
But then it does, as we squeeze hours into moments.

Teach me how to write your name,
what it means to glide in dreams,
how simple it is to be complex,
and after the mind, the heart naturally flows.

Then give me strength to draw a secret out—
that I never want to let go—and earth
turns pink, and orange, then starry, before us,
and I'm filled like the moon with your glow.

III
INVOLVE ME IN HAPPENINGS

And since you know you cannot see yourself, so well as by reflection, I, your glass, will modestly discover to yourself, that of yourself which you yet know not of.

—William Shakespeare

FLYING LESSONS

Too high except for birds to reach,
I act like a tune in attempts to confuse.
Problems look smaller, amid the leaves.
I might give up this madness to spite me.

Pay no attention, little birds,
I'm just another whistle among singers.
No need to poke out my eyes and devour my seed.
I'll not consider your parts, as if quartered.

I still see myself in you, flying.
Calls don't sound blue from up here, so much.
Such wingspans are common in my mind,
lines and spaces leave quite a lot to get away with.

I'd just as soon revere the nest in all its emptiness,
than peer through a window into some dark hope,
and have myself known as wind's dreamer.
For in life, we stay wild when we can't believe.

There's so much more I'd like to conceal—
how I harden like ice, just to melt and flow free,
and feel sorry for this primitive truth.
God, give it to me! And oh yes, God, I am falling.

By two I'm expecting to end the night hammered.
I already hate tomorrow, until dark again.
I just keep going back to, damn, where I love it,
where there's one thought to go till the hand meets the head.

SPINNING

A tiny spider on a ceiling sees no similar creature in sight,
but keeps searching, because life is a process, not an entity.

Not *mine* so much as a point of view.
Take this line, and make it more about itself.

That tiny spider's counterpart exists,
so its purpose in wandering fills a void.

It believes in another, and moves—
how pure is that?

A coexistence of experience
on a pleasure pain continuum.

When candlelight comes to mind,
and no other life is, I share an illusion.

Happiness is a balancing act for fire.
There is loneliness in hope.

Yet I long to touch you with a word.
That possibility is the best almost existing.

Emotions sway into moonlight, reeling,
refusing to compromise themselves.

These are the dreams, combating for truces.
As for questions, an answer,

but no one to notice.
Let me move you, or we've wasted time.

ADJUSTING THE LONELINESS

I hear a faucet drip into its puddle, grown to capacity,
striving to avoid stagnation, just to know its own emotion,
in the middle with itself, like a trinity.
The goal of essence is overflowing.
Ultimate unity is not enough for even an ocean.
It sways back and forth at the sky, as if into a mirror,
reflecting itself in the deep dark light.
Reground me, engulf me, elate me, drown me,
I can't get enough without passing out.
The sun never goes down, we rise up
Like mountains in the north block time;
Up in clouds, that flirt with poetry and roses,
Become this scribble, revealed elapsing.
Bring sandpipers and baby's breath
like a tear refracting colors makes a sound.
Strong as waves I gaze between.
Shore is more of an end than it seems—
the first drop is deepest, the last licks the surface;
I remain with the wind, evolved in motion,
orchestrating silence into dreams of reality;
There are chances, and odds, and fates say we meet,
there are preconceived notions, rivers and gatherings,
there are miles between and limitless faces,
there are endless lines but I can wait.

THE SOUL AT HOME

As I sit looking out my window
at the window across the street
no one looks back at me.
Strange place for a window, so high,
perhaps serving only the purpose of light.

But as its blinds, so obviously human and
apparently proud to be seen through
shudder slightly in the breeze,
it occurs to me that I don't feel anything
because my window isn't even open.

I get up and open it, simple enough, but
when I sit back down the mood is changed
from one of isolation to involvement.
Days seem to idle a bit more alive,
or at least, life outside seems to be going by.

But I'm still just a house to a world on the street,
nothing more than a symbol of what
every automatic driver taking snapshots of a river
already knows. That in fact, they're not even drivers,
just cars passing by the memory of a house.

CLOCKWATCHING

Forty minutes to stay, or go.
No chance to get to the bones, I must decide.
This ache I attribute to waiting alone,
but I can't give up already.

For faith, I find fault with creation.
Blame a stone, my disease of a mind.
I don't care about law, screw you and your motion,
I'm reading Shakespeare.

Fear the poet in you, son, I warn you.
It appears to need mixing up, and that never slows
until you're dizzy, passing out.
Besides, nothing's left to write.

Only twenty-four minutes remain.
There's no stopping now from coming.
Should I listen to a song, or what?
I decide to be bored, I have time.

Is forward to the dreams belief?
The psychos tell me flawlessness is myth.
I keep searching for what to throw away,
the way the dead hoped for a moment.

Ask no questions, be precise,
describe your moment like nobody else.
Our feelings are only close, inexact humanity.
Still five minutes but I'm not going.

CLOCKWATCHING AGAIN

I'm not a poet for any sad reason.
I crave more than God knows, and confuse myself.
I'd tear a secret to shreds here,
the wrist sees Karma as a blade.

To your tenderness, the hard parts.
Truth about anything makes a sound.
Like that in an instant the deadline's arisen.
I empty the trash, and am writing about it.

Time goes spreading itself out.
The hour hands are fractions,
in such slow motion it's not even eight,
and I'm halfway to tomorrow again.

What do I know? Do you see how long it takes
to figure out what I'm thinking?
I want poetry like bodies to warm me,
at the bottom, until the rhythm's spent.

LINES LEADING NOWHERE

Do I seem down, my resurrected?
I'm unintentionally lost in this imagined likelihood of light.
Remember, I'm here to punish the dream, you, to honor the lie,
not to kid every whim ever known through the ages.

How I've longed to be mystical being like you were,
lacking your shinier halves of faces,
with every stinking rule bent by legitimate replacements.
Preoccupations can't be understated.

There appear to be ends we need to be out there,
to maintain stand-by philosophies, but then,
when's the last time you asked a poet anything?
Unwritten law, we wonder into midnight, scribbling.

There are things that I think when I see what I see,
adjusting goals to conform to the line.
You would think such a thing must be true, but it isn't,
a mosquito disguised as madness enters the blind.

There are different ways of being an animal.
Now I stare into the stew, back at the eyes of a potato,
whisper to the ears of corn, get into the head of lettuce,
break the heart of an artichoke.

Cooling favors open space,
burning for no other purpose than heat.
Prepared to pay our way in smoke,
the world is still that way today.

The first clock bears the arms of Venus de Milo,
but she makes her point much better without them.
It just gets me more ticked off as I talk.
The so-called quotation marks get a dose of their own medicine.

What of the turning aside? Meteoric
giants, in the past, debated the relevance of relevance.
There was no point, they determined,
and no speaker ever content with his thoughts.

INSTINCT

I want the most truth ever told in a single line.
Everything before now is dead.
I could fill myself in with symbols and get used to it.
Paste stars here moment by moment,
cast a glow in dark scorpion, and let it mean me.
Time's out to kill so let's put this in motion.
All our lives change because of a moth,
with its no less difficult form of thinking.
My first thought is to strike it down.
Second, that it *feels* the same way I do,
flying into walls, and lights.
Third, let it be and write about it.
Fourth, for sake of symmetry.
It appears I can no longer stop, so I go on,
but why do you listen?
I dement the future with circumstance.
You are tomorrow's being, overjoyed.
Well be warned, there's pain,
and it knows you completely,
that you do this rather than scream,
prefer the night go unrevealed,
so your face won't be in your hands like mine.
The idols dwindle,
and hesitate to estimate the fraction which remains.
You phantom, you've been named.
You may as well turn to stone
as be concealed in demeanor,
to be included in your own existence,
a master of distraction,
an answer to some generic question like who, or why.
Then go out to the fence of meaning and decay.

To be God next time makes me devil now.
A list wherein you mention a name no one's heard,
so they look around the room
in suspicious search for non-existence.
We need presence to believe in,
and when there's none we waiver
like church laws on palimpsest,
making ourselves up as we go along.

IV
HUMBLED

He hoped and prayed that there wasn't an afterlife. Then he realized there was a contradiction involved here and merely hoped that there wasn't an afterlife.
—Douglas Adams

What I Would Say to God Right Now

You really do know how to get me to think.
Yes, I am grateful for our words,
and the places they come from.

Love the eye swells that they leave,
even if I don't know why,
because the feelings traveled far.

I keep rising from the ashes with a name,
like a thousand Adams,
until I'm torn apart with voices.

Forgive me for what I have done to myself,
and for what I am about to do.
I am addicted, and these words are in on it.

I knew you by logic but now I must touch you.
There had to be some explanation for the emptiness.
I was wrong to think I could create you.

Like I could absorb you as much as I tried.
We are two snakes swallowing each other
and ending up alone.

Just give me a little light to shed.
Let me leave this life all at once but the words to linger.
Send a spiral down my spine.

God, I am writing, make yourself known here.
Pluck a particle from air,
show these people what we mean.

I want to give you what I can, for dust.
Please acknowledge my existence.
Or do I have to die to reach you?

What God Says

I.
Now, when it's late, you begin to see through me.
I'm not sure when the first time was, you fell
from my tongue-crafted heights back to earth.

You have touched the depths of yourself without me.
When the muse becomes poet, where do I turn?
Gone off, as usual, in search of the spiral,

Met with no imagination,
Torn like Cinna for his verses,
grief defeats euphoria too, when you tell me goodbye.

I have waned with the moon,
hung over into a workday,
where is the blessing in that?

I feel dreamt away, dissolute,
why do you mourn me?
I'd sooner remain an island than have you ever cry for my sake,

to be touched in mind only, from afar,
in a fitful impasse, diminishing.
I'll still desire you for this.

How I've ridden the vortex and spun
in spite of gravity over the drain,
just to pull you down with me into reality.

For I cannot really fly, and hot blood flows through me.
I am a name to be uttered in a distant language.
How many times must I resurrect myself, how many can I?

There's nothing else but to lay in the dust or get up.
We entered the night in need of a song.
For your whisper, I'll dance with you forever.

II.
Keep searching.
Thought is a matter of tense,
so your poetry is dead for having seen me.

What do you expect?
You never notice the many miracles
experienced every day,

The beating heart, invisible breath.
The very light in which you see amazes
flowers in their beds and dreamers where they lay.

Even odd whispers interrupt, but you ignore them.
It takes days to discover truth and forever to reveal it,
so these lines should have meaning for someone alone.

I seek your love, and doubt myself,
for there's this sound and every other.
Thank you, for this prayer.

There is innocence about you.
I've seen the truth and mistaken it.
But I never say anything you don't already know.

As for your eyes looking back, they are a stream
from which life flows, and overwhelms me.
I could fall into your glow, disintegrate.

Let me breathe into you part of me,
so I can know what it feels like to be revealed.
Forgive another dream, my creation,

but it is night, and I'm alone.
We can be each other's maker.
You will thank me for these words, believe me.

My Addiction

I stay up late, affecting tomorrow.
Lust can't make me forget manzanita again.
Reveal myself to me, become my reflection.

Let me fondle charlotte russe, emerged in cream, so
I can feel my fingers be music, bent back, in discovery,
strain concealed in their beat.

Belief is on its deathbed with a question for the end.
So here we go again, relapsing.
Let us wade into the hallowed self a feeling at a time.

Mar the reflection in ripple, blue magician.
Is it hope coming back, or another trick?
Fragrant, I imagine, disappearing into one of us.

AMBITION

I am poet.
Silky hair and other attributes.
Earthbound, working an English
in which words suffer themselves.

At night starts the longing.
No life but emotion and count.
Manipulate the air to breathe.
A planet slow at viewing starlight.

We read ancient text, trace languages back,
blow gently the dust off of carved, toothbrushed curves.
Figure sound out, develop translations. Gesture.
Still speak sign. That's how I want my life to be.

So through the mind
I greet thee fully, as if we stand beside ourselves.
Perceive a bit of animal persona.
Split quick, turn-happy, aware of other treasures in the canyon.

We come trickling down earth's side, gathered to spring.
Its world tipped beneath the tap, a goldfish clings to its gravel
and castle against the urgent need to learn to walk or else.
One finds it simpler to stay in the bowl then get used to dirt.

V
THE TITLE LIED

He was one of those men who think that the world can be saved by writing a pamphlet.

—Benjamin Disraeli

PRECISION

I like theme songs that get to the point.
Gilligan's Island told a tale.
I don't want to hear a tale.
You're stranded, that's that.

The Brady Bunch had a story.
I don't care about a story.
The Flintstones from Bedrock,
who gives a damn?

But "meet George Jetson" is concise.
"His boy Elroy." Of course, what else?
"Daughter Judy" is efficiency at its finest.
"Jane his wife" and the song is over.

It's as good as it gets in eleven words.
You sing your songs and I'll sing mine.
If silence was a word, I'd use it.
And it would still be here when I finished.

THE CREATOR

This may be my last emotion.
But shall I introduce the light, and make it plain?
It grows sacred, fanning itself for a breath.

I have told you of the pain,
how it needs us to exist
and is the cause of all we do.

Appease pain or die is the very first rule.
How like a steel river, it still moves,
so one can only brush against it,

to merely sip from its life and find beauty.
What a ponderous dream to be bearing a soul.
You throwback from an outcry, wonder.

What blessed Messiah? Christen this.
Come through or don't wake me up again.
You're it. Oh, and pain's passionate, baby,

grows genius in flicking to liquid the stone,
pounds like teeth into musk and grinds the bone
until we're swollen from the hole and kept alive.

See? Pain knows, is of infinite patience and degree.
The natural man has little hope but to fear forever.
The Lord of feeling is the poet who does me in.

God, I ache because of you, and still want more.
But I can't stand it.
There goes my last emotion, burning out.

EVENTS TO THIS POEM

1.

This had to be where I am at this moment
Cut off at Oak, the seconds I waited
With these very particular moods and sensations
The positioning sun with its moons and its clouds
Its clocks and its circles all wending about

Other men had to be driving then too
Home to take their immediate showers
Note the ominous noose on the family tree's
Verisimilar strain through my literal line

If mind is fashioned to environment, every inch of mine is paved
Its roads don't lead to glitter town though
But are named after trees removed in the making
And all will be stranding me, moments from now
On the outskirts of the empty page

2.

So downward the spiral, gnashing and clawing
Drowned in reality, wanting a name
No mind that conjures such gray fascinations
While fashioning syllables otherwise shapeless
Escapes inasmuch as there's anyone watching

But having once mentioned complete anonymity
Abandons to dangle on motionless longing
An untenable utterance wrought with ambition
Comparing its worth to the smoke, as it lingers

Where is the light bearer musing its lullabies
Incanting soliloquies tested till blameless?
What were formerly grunts strung together like baubles
Now polished no less than an ape when its shaven
Resigning to fear in its vacant reflection

3.

Before facing our problem, I tried simply fading
Mustering keenly a murmuring whir
Having lusted to hold your distractions against me
In those song-seeking days now severely deflated
Over uncounted midnights in perfect disguises

While the sun carved its emptiness into my patience
Hands shook with my shadow, and spine undermining
Daydreams of wordplay, remarkable phrases
By mere technicalities grown civilized

As persona refrains these most grave explanations
For things about which you may not even care
Remember again that we're in this together
And consumed nonetheless by leprous deadlines
Keep expiring in pieces, two at a time

4.

I burnt up whole evenings and portions of others
In bargains with language for something to say
While my muses litigious, having all become editors
Downtown in their skyscrapers charge me for waiting
Typically, at the appointed hour, the hostess prognosticates further delay

On the phone to a voice with a name recognizable
Crossing out letters and mangling phrases
Arises the unexpected diversion
Inking final adjustments without validation

As if in a twinkling her possessions obtain me
After only the corpse of pure thinking remains
In a box wrapped in plastic, the genie I buried
Beneath motions appealing and templates of pleadings
Proving vapors don't vanish, they transform into stains

5.
After this, I'll look for the real beginning
The one that's projected a heartbeat away
From undisclosed cases, so desperate to harm you
Wildly lashing, fallen from faith
Memories corrupted, forsaken, waylaid

Unfatalistically, cells in an instant
Are throughout unobserved revolutions replaced
Yesterday's sandcastle trickles to windblown
Like a worm through the hole of an hourglass waist

From lines interwoven and waxing fantastic, instinctively
Broken, concocted of schemes, to big bangs and present pencil
Gyrations, let somebody brighter than I am attend
To mixing red stars grounded into fine powders
With water to mimic the blood they once shed

WATER

I'm in between laws and dark places again,
in the shadows of cold, still surfaces,
where the water is sky's reflection.

Even after it gets in the air, it falls and won't stop running.
Swirls like thinking or gets stagnant.
Earth is only part of where it comes from.

It comes from illusion's condensation,
from the icicles, from the snow.
from swallowing whole and waving goodbye.

I didn't mean to be so abrupt.
I meant to say more, I meant to listen.
I meant for you to speak my words, and taste me.

But here we are another line down across an ocean.
One dreams, the other prays,
wanting into each other like razors.

TELLING TIME BY THE SHADOWS

1.
Begin with this most basic assertion:
I am hollow, unredeemed.
I fell, am falling still, into deepest suspense,

where indelible emotion continues nonetheless to gnaw.
I carve its initials in the bark of a dog.
I etch its name upon the water.

What of the missing hair?
Spiders use it for webs, while under the table,
the legs are consumed by termites.

2.

The fear of the mirror is merely a name
I give myself, then take away.
The magic diluted in the voice of someone nearing.

Such is the image surrendered to plain observation,
painted by numbers, the distance in a cup unfolded.
Too often my reflection mumbles, lacking the confidence of poetry,

it faces no one, looks the other way,
and begs itself to comprehend
some meaning in the empty space.

3.

Driving to work, I think about you,
our paths crossing momentarily as we move in opposite directions.
Such is the way chance pushes me lately.

I chip away at hours, six stories high,
looking toward the coast at endless gray,
following a lonely scent toward unseen destinations.

Understand the path that leads me doesn't know what it's about,
can't see the light, if it's been shone,
the dust falls back to spite the bone.

4.
Tonight the very moon is blue.
It shines behind clouds where I can't even see it, as do you.
I summon the wind to nudge you into sight.

Though I climb the most sky-felt mountain,
the moon keeps moving farther away.
Not even the sun can uncover the void.

Only the clouds can spill their rain like words upon a page,
while those it dreams to touch run inside,
remembering the beat of someone knocking.

5.

The sun is a father that eats its own children.
A star that extracts its tax daily in flesh,
all the spine-wrenching night keeps turning its back.

As givers of life go, it's a deceiver.
The sun would set the earth on fire.
As we speak, the sun is hanging,

casting shadows of feet ten times their size.
Its goal is equilibrious stone,
to render earth's tear drop that skull of a moon.

6.

Another name for lunacy is what we need,
applied to the hue of clandestine appeals to the winding.
I'd sooner be high than underground, but on the earth to flailing.

The very tide kisses the shore at random,
planets spin for want of anything else to do,
would it really seem so out of place if I were drawn to you?

Your presence stands like stone against the wind,
while mine dissipates like vapor
into the drunkenness of the dream of someone staring into night.

7.

A few naked words consuming poisons
cause the irony of birth,
while everything around me dies, and I say *nothing*.

It's hard, you know, it's tough,
the feeling seems to be too much fright to overcome,
without worry of a heart collapsed, or thinking I should call it age.

Weep with me now for a dream long lost.
Leave me reeling from the pain. Teach me what it means to pray,
and why the vein can love the blade.

8.
Unafraid is tragedy,
almost hard for me to speak, you were so right.
Near to smiling is the breeze,

a Mona Lisa of unpredictability,
aware it can't go on forever,
pointing the way to oblivious faces, convincing no one.

The whiteness of the page is glaring,
the letters, for now, just shadows,
pretending to be solid as the truth, which never fades.

9.
The greenery knows full well the fall.
The very branches ache under weight of fruitful gain.
The sound of crackling fire known to ashes, not to trees.

There is a warmth, an afterglow.
So signal the stars, and everything beneath
within my head, when I remember.

Not that I forget! But time is decay, and little else.
As any flame is fading, you are the wind,
recalling the mortar of which the pedestal is made.

10.
Here's what I've been trying to explain:
There is no reason in all the world
why a moth should be drawn to a flame.

Not every creature of the dark seeks light.
Most are stalking easy prey,
so phosphorous eyes better know when to close.

The intimacy of truth is just amazing.
Every path tireless in unrealized beginnings,
Making any point ascend to every dangler of strings in different ways.

MEDICINE

I remember the sound of dreaming,
the tiger, the arrow, the voices, the stars,
and still soak in the meaning.

Eyes cover the goal of existence.
I want my soul back.
I think I left my body too.

Dowse me in misbelieved meaning,
unforeseen magic, ancestral devotion.
Control events, alter consciousness,

let language tear me to pieces.
Divine the hidden, teach me to feel.
Reveal me on a different level.

I've studied night and here's the deal:
it's rough seeing anything perfect.
How did I get here is the question.

I think too often of creation,
the lowest common denominator,
at love's worst, hoping for glimpses.

I see wind move in pieces, moments, others, even less.
This line could be about *you*, believe me.
At least I could offer some proof as to nothing.

Sway, all you mothers of God, for emotion,
Sway, all you on your knees praying.
Sway, you twisted musicians and lavender fields,

for ocean, pulse, and pain crave passion.
Words bent on angels, reverb, circle higher,
disappear like shadows into light, and make me wonder.

We will dream, at least I will, of nameless surprises,
but until life rises from its likeness,
may we heal one another.

Printed in the United States
201852BV00002B/1-324/P